Greenhill Books

G.I. VICTORY

Overleaf:
PFCs Vernon H. Bradberry and Robert
L. Mims, MPs, stand guard in front of
the Remagen/Ling bridge on the Rhine
River, 1945.

G. I. VICTORY

The U.S. Army in World War II Color

Jeffrey L. Ethell and David C. Isby

Greenhill Books
London

Stackpole Books
Pennsylvania

Greenhill Books

This edition of *G.I. Victory* first published 2003 by Greenhill Books, Lionel Leventhal
Limited, Park House, 1 Russell Gardens, London NW11 9NN
and
Stackpole Books, 5067 Ritter Road, Mechanicsburg, PA 17055, USA

British Library Cataloguing in Publication Data
Ethell, Jeffrey
G.I. victory – (Greenhill Military Paperback)
United States. Army – History – World War, 1939–1945 – Pictorial works
United States. Marine Corps– World War, 1939–1945 – Pictorial works
World War, 1939–1945 – Campaigns – Pictorial works
I. Title
940.5'4'0973'0222
ISBN 1-85367-570-9

Library of Congress Cataloging-in-Publication Data available

Designed and edited by DAG Publications Ltd.
Designed by David Gibbons; edited by Philip Jarrett; layout by Anthony A Evans.
Origination by Master Image, Singapore. Printed and bound in China by Imago.

Photograph Credits

Calvin Bannon, 134; Mark H. Brown/USAFA, 155; Dennis Glen Cooper, 43; J. P. Crowder via
Dorothy Helen Crowder, 11; Arnold M. Delmonico, 72, 150; Maurice Eppstein, 132;
George J. Fleury, 124, 133; Robert Frizell via Kenneth Kailey, 63; F M. Grove, 73; Frederick
H. Hill, 125, 127, 129, 130, 136,140,141; Norman W. Jackson, 44; Wilbur Kuhn via Mrs
Wilbur Kuhn, 128, 139; via Randy Liebermann, 5, 6, 7, 8, 28, 29; John L. Lowden, 111, 112;
Chuck Miles via Evelyn Miles, 36, 37; via Stan Pet, 9; Louis Raburn, 10; Alexander C. Sloan,
102, 154; Spitzer, 135; USAF 18,46; James G. Weir, 131; Stanley J. Wyglendowski,
153. All other photographs are from the US National Archives.

Contents

The Authors

The late Jeff Ethell wrote over the course of his career more than fifty books on military history, primarily dealing with aviation, including *Wings of War* and many other books featuring rare World War II color images. His father taught him to fly before he learned to drive a car. He logged over 4,200 hours in more than 200 different types of aircraft, from World War I fighters to modern jets. He served as an on-screen host and scriptwiter for numerous television documentaries and was the military correspondent for ABC's *Wide World of Flying* video series. He was killed in an airplane crash in 1997.

David C. Isby is a Washington-based attorney and consultant on national security and foreign affairs issues. He has written or edited twenty books and over three hundred articles and essays and designed 19 conflict simulations. He has frequently appeared in the media, has lectured widely at staff colleges, and has appeared before congressional committees as an independent expert. A former legislative assistant in the House of Representatives and an editor of *Strategy & Tactics* magazine, he is also a private pilot.

Introduction

The 1941–45 US Army soldier became known as the G.I., from the abbreviation for Government Issue, the source of equipment, clothing and weapons. Winston Churchill called the US Army of the Second World War a 'prodigy of organization'. Comprising some 174,000 men as Europe moved towards war in 1939, it was 8,300,000 strong at the time of victory in 1945.

This increase in size was matched by a commensurate increase in effectiveness. In 1939 the US Army was unfit for modern warfare. By 1945 it had mastered the atomic bomb, the jet engine and instantaneous global communications. The speed with which the army transformed itself, was sent into battle, learned from its experience, and finally defeated all of its enemies provides an outstanding example of leadership and organization.

The US Army of 1941-45 was an industrial-age force. It was the era of mass production, and countless photographs show the same equipment – the Sherman tank, the jeep, the 2½-ton truck and the LST (landing ship tank) – reflecting the strength of the industrial base and its successes at production. The strength of this approach was reflected in the plenitude of *matériel* upon which the G.I. relied, arousing the amazement of his enemies and the envy of his allies. Yet even this finest of industrial-age achievements had its limitations. The Shermans did not evolve fast enough to meet a changing threat. Planned wartime production seriously underestimated the number of LSTs required. In both their strengths and weaknesses, the G.I.'s weapons and equipment reflected America.

Through the medium of contemporary color photography, this book aims to set out the story of the G.I.s themselves, some of the equipment they used, the conditions under which they served and the victory they won. Kodachrome was in its infancy during the Second World War, but Americans had seen how it could be used in the pages of magazines such as *National Geographic, LIFE* and, once they were overseas, the British *Picture Post.*

The images themselves come from a mixture of official and amateur photographers. Both suffered from a shortage of suitable color film and, more significantly, processing, which could then only be done by Kodak. Kodachrome had improved greatly in the years immediately before the war, from the slow color film of the 1930s, which had difficulty capturing anything other than static subjects and tended to present murky colors, to wartime Kodachrome with an ASA rating of 10, which required good natural lighting. Many photographers, both amateur and professional, continued to prefer black-and-white film, which seemed (and to many still seems) the most expressive way of depicting modern war.

An advantage – or disadvantage – of the relative scarcity of Second World War Army color photography is that the photos are spread unevenly through the vast US Army, and concentrate on the spots where someone had a camera full of color film. This allows the photographs to focus in depth where they cannot offer breadth. The July 1941 California maneuvers, the 7th Armored Division's fighting around St. Vith in the Battle of the Bulge, the 92nd Infantry Division's combat engineers clearing mines on an Italian beach and the first glider troops over the Rhine are all present in multiple images.

The old cliché says that every picture tells a story. In these photographs there are usually many stories in each image. The equipment depicted ranges from the simple improvised snow camouflage suit sewn from mattress covers by seamstresses in Nancy, and seen here worn by Sgt Doug Dillard of the 551st Parachute Infantry, to large and complex specialized armored vehicles. The emphasis on uniforms and food reflects two of the abiding concerns of the soldier in the field – staying comfortable and keeping fed.

Another story revolves around the units involved. Despite the army's insistence on standardization, they all had not only their own stories, but their own strengths and weaknesses. Where a photograph falls in a unit's part in the great victory is indeed another story. The units depicted in these photographs are a representative cross-section of the Army Ground Forces, Army Service Forces and elements of the Army Air Forces, and include many of the army's most famous divisions; 1st Armored, 1st Infantry, 7th Armored, 7th Infantry, 36th Infantry and 82nd Airborne among others. In some cases this was just luck. In others, official photographers knew that these divisions were likely to be found where the action was.

The stories of the events themselves are also told in the photographs. The G.I.s propped up against supply canisters are actually the first glider pilots and troops across the Rhine, having arrived only hours before in CG-4A gliders (in operational terms, the nearest thing to a winged coffin that American soldiers ever volunteered to fly in) by landing in fields infested with anti-aircraft guns. The story lies in how they ended up waiting next to that railroad line, rather than in the details of the photographs themselves.

Perhaps the most interesting story, however, is G.I. life, in and out of combat. These photographs of daily surroundings could be the postcard-like evidence of European cities visited on leave, the exotic sights of Pacific islands; all attracted the use of color film. There are also daily events – the chow line, the mess kit supper of corned beef hash – which were then commonplace but are now fading in memory.

Finally, there are the portraits of people whose significance represents their place and time. Patton and MacArthur are here, but these are the only 'stars'. The other faces are representative. Although they are not immediately identifiable, they show us that the massive wartime army was, like all of America, made up of diverse individuals. Now that even the youngest Second World War G.I. is elderly, these color photographs are becoming increasingly important in showing those too young for the great crusade just how the world appeared through their eyes during the years 1941 to 1945.

These photographs provide an interesting though peripheral view of the G.I.'s allies and enemies. The British, French, Poles, Chinese, Italian partisans – and the Marine Corps – all made interesting subjects for the camera. The number of photographs in which US and Royal Navy landing craft appear, especially the invaluable LSTs, are a reminder that many G.I.s spent much time at sea, on their way to new theaters or beachheads.

A more limited view of the enemy appears. Bodies, prisoners, refugees or, most often, wrecked equipment is what the G.I. saw of those he had traveled halfway around the world to vanquish, and this is reflected in the photographs. Real combat is also in these photographs, but at a distance. The artillery on the next ridge line on Saipan, and the blast of a demolition charge on Bougainville, are seen from a distance, where the photographer could have his camera in hand, rather than an M1 rifle, without risking his life. But this, as the combat soldier will attest, is how they normally saw it themselves. The enemy was seen only fleetingly on the battlefield, if at all.

The scope and breadth of these images reflect the massive size of the wartime army and the significance of its accomplishment. There is something in this collection to touch on almost everything the G.I.s did. The US Army was, and remains, primarily an institution existing for the purpose of killing people that need to be killed and destroying things that need to be destroyed. There is ample evidence in these photographs that, if they were never as efficient as some, they were certainly effective at doing this. But these pictures also show the old Okinawan woman being helped to the rear, where she will doubtless find food and shelter. The demobilized Japanese soldier driving his oxcart will find that the US Army will impose a regime that, far from oppressing him, will make him a citizen of a democratic, peaceful and prosperous land.

Other achievements of the wartime US Army are hinted at. The many photographs of evacuation and care of the wounded reminds us that no army ever before took such care of its own men or made such advances in medicine. Often more welcome than more abstract freedoms, G.I. medicine brought antibiotics to many – Americans, civilians and enemies alike – who would otherwise have died. The G.I. reading a paperback book is a reminder that a generation was trained and educated both in uniform and in post-service higher education. The experience of wartime service transformed Americans, just as the war itself transformed America. But it is hard to argue with the judgment of Samuel Stouffer, who wrote in his classic three-volume study of the wartime army, *The American Soldier*; 'Though our armies crossed all the seas and lived on all the continents, the men ... came home as they went out, indubitably American'.

Not all of the stories contained in these photographs are positive. The army's tactics were often inadequate, and were refined only after costly combat lessons; its weapons were often inferior in performance to those of its opponents; and its treatment of its own soldiers too often reflected the worst rather than the best elements of American society as a whole. These photos show useless little light tanks in service at a time when the panzer divisions were already deadly efficient and well armed. The ration boxes and track links used as improvised glacis armor on Sherman tanks, are reminders that the military bureaucracy often let down the men who had to do the fighting, whether in tanks vulnerable to enemy shells or in boots that were a standing invitation to frostbite. African-American and women G.I.s appear in significant but peripheral roles, underlining the changes in America over the 50 years since victory, the impetus for many coming from the shared experience of service in 1941–45.

The US Army did, however, deliver the one single important thing it was asked for – victory – in 1945. Where the US Army stood, the Red Army, despite its own great victories, could not set foot. With the brilliant light of hindsight, the victory gained in 1945 paved the way for another victory, that in the Cold War 45 years later.

Jeffrey Ethell writes: The treasure trove of World War II color images in this book represents one of those 'instant' success stories that took twenty years and hundreds of people to make happen. My first efforts at publishing vintage military color as the subject of an entire book were supported and produced by Greenhill's Lionel Leventhal when he was in charge of Arms and Armour Press. I pitched the idea to him and in 1983 we did two paperback volumes in the Warbirds Illustrated series called *American Warplanes: World War II to Korea.* In the ensuing ten years we talked about doing a large hardback book, but not until the fiftieth anniversary of World War II and my collecting thousands of wartime Kodachrome slides did we jump in again with *Wings of War.* He wanted yet another book, so with his persistent questions about my doing the US Army in wartime color I gave in. He teamed me with David Isby, and the result is *G.I. Victory,* the only full-color look at the ground war in print.

Needless to say, I am indebted to the many veterans and historians who shared their color with me: Stan Piet, Rabdy Liebermann, Louis Raburn, Dorothy Helen Crowder for her late husband Jeep's slides, Evelyn Miles for her late husband Chuck's slides, Dennis Glen Cooper, Norman W. Jackson, Kenneth Kailey for providing the late Robert Frizell's slides, Arnold N. Delmonico, F. M. Grove, Alexander C. Sloan, John L. Lowden. George J. Fleury, Frederick H. Hill, James G. Weir, Maurice Eppstein, Bill Bielauskas for introducing me to Calvin Bannon's slides, Stanley J. Wyglendowski, and Duane J. Reed at the US Air Force Academy for allowing me to copy the Mark Brown collection. Those images without a specific credit came from the excellent National Archives holdings through the generosity of Betry Hill, Head of the Still Picture Branch.

From the inception of the project, David Isby enthusiastically came on board as my co-author. A leading expert in his field, he quickly sorted out what was going on where to whom by looking at each slide through a loop, spotting shoulder patches, obscure vehicle markings and other very small details. Many of these images were simply shot without time to take down the specifics of units, dates or locations... this was no barrier to David, who sat down and wrote outstanding commentary to each photograph. The book, quite simply, would not have been done without him. We hope you enjoy this as much as we have enjoyed creating it.

David Isby writes: I would like to thank my parents, Joseph Isby (who was in the Great Crusade as a USAAF NCO and C-47 navigator) and Peggy Carpenter Isby (British governmental service and war industries as an administrator), who went through the photos Jeff Ethell had so diligently assembled to give me the benefit of their memories.

Jeff Ethell's encyclopedic knowledge of Second World War color photography made this whole project possible. Color photography presents the reader with the view closest to those who actually saw the events. By assembling a collection of these photographs, large enough to compare and contrast with each other; he has created an invaluable, unique historical record.

The most important acknowledgement is to those who actually took the photographs, whether official or amateur photographers, and those who appeared in them, whether carefully posed or candidly snapped. Jeff Ethell collected the photos, I wrote the words, and Lionel Leventhal put the whole between two covers, but it is really their book and we have tried to show a little of the world at war as they saw it. The list of credits acknowledges the photographers in the few cases where these are known. For all the others, please accept our gratitude not only for the photographs, but for what you did fifty years ago.

This revised edition was prepared without Jeff Ethell's participation, for he tragically died in the crash of a restored Second World War P-38 fighter plane in 1997. A man of great learning and humor, with a strong faith that he kept in his heart, he is missed by all those who had the privilege of working with him. Corrections to the original edition were gratefully received from Brent Bevan, Guiseppe Francesconi, Paul L. James, Ian Philips, Stephen "Cookie" Sewell, and Steven Zaloga.

Jeffrey L. Ethell, Front Royal, VA, 1995
David C. Isby, Washington, D.C., 2003

The Army Before
Pearl Harbor

1. (previous page) Military Policemen fall in for inspection before going on guard duty in 1941, wearing the M1917 helmets, wool service coats and canvas leggings of the pre-war army. Physical security against sabotage in the United States was a major concern in 1940-42. With hindsight, this emphasis seems near-hysterical, but at the time memories of German sabotage in the First World War – especially the devastating 'Black Tom' explosion – as well as the social disruption that accompanied the First World War in the United States, were very real. The MPs are armed with the M1928A1 Thompson .45 caliber submachine-gun, which they would use throughout the war.

2. An unarmed M2A2/A3 light tank fords a stream during exercises in the summer of 1941. Obsolete and technically inadequate compared with the tanks in combat in Europe, it nevertheless provided useful training, especially in the prewar exercises, giving many US commanders skills they would be able to apply to better tanks. One of the units in these maneuvers, the 192nd Tank Battalion, was then shipped to the Philippines, and was re-equipped with M3 light tanks before going into action against the invading Japanese in December 1941.

3. The Coast Artillery, like the Air Corps, was one of the 'high-technology' branches of the pre-war Army, providing much of the cadre for massive expansion of the air defense artillery in 1940-42. Here, 'cosmoliners' (the nickname came from the preservative grease that the Coast Artillerymen lathered on their equipment) in the new M1 steel helmets (adopted by the US Army Infantry Board in 1940 but first introduced into service in 1941), and with old-style triangular gas mask containers under their arms, practise gun drill on 12in M1912 coastal mortars. While more modern weapons used naval-style power rammers, the shells for the M1912s were trundled from the ready ammunition storage on antique carts and manually rammed, as seen here. The bagged powder charges, being held off to the side, would follow as soon as the shells were rammed home. The weapons were used in action in the Philippines in 1942, and remained in service in the United States and its territories throughout the war.

4. Coast Artillerymen prepare an 8in Mk VI coast gun, mounted on a railroad flatcar, for action by pushing away its storage shed, camouflaged as an ocean-front bungalow, on the California coast on 30 July 1943. Only at Astoria, Oregon, were the coast defenses of the continental United States challenged by enemy warships; a Japanese submarine surfaced to bombard oil storage tanks in 1942.

5. The 53rd Infantry Regiment of the 7th Infantry Division participates in the July 1941 California Maneuvers in the Salinas Valley. Neither the troops nor their commanders were used to the large-scale tactical movement of trucks, as exercised here. A dog is waiting to board a truck with the troops on the left. 'There is probably no camp or post in the Army which does not have at least one dog,' wrote Private William Saroyan in 1943.

6. On 12 July 1941, troops of the 'Red' forces have supper during the July 1941 California exercise. A stateside touch is provided by the loaves of fresh white bread from a local bakery; in the field overseas, 'B' rations would be prepared by unit kitchens. 'B' rations accounted for 80 per cent of all meals consumed by the army in Northwest Europe and Italy, the remainder being 'C' and 'K' rations.

7. A pre-war-model Willys jeep (then often called a 'peep') of the southern 'Red' forces on exercises in California's Salinas Valley on 14 July 1941. These exercises were important in evaluating new equipment such as the jeep and the SCR-171 radio, and in introducing the massive intakes of new troops and formations –draftees, volunteers and federalized National Guardsmen alike – to the realities of modern mechanized combat. The exercises also helped army leadership to think in these same modern terms, shaking them out of the pre-war 'garrison mentality'.

8. The post-exercise critique at Jolon, near the Salinas Valley, California, on 21 July 1941. These exercises pitted the 7th Infantry Division against the IX Corps (including the 40th Infantry Division, originally part of the California National Guard, now federalized), demonstrating the skills of Major General Joseph W. Stilwell, the 7th's commander, whose ability to be abrasive had earned him the nickname 'Vinegar Joe'. In September Stilwell also did well in the multi-corps exercise, when the Fourth Army took on IX Corps.

9. The largest pre-war exercises were the GHQ Carolina maneuvers of November 1941. Here, a troop of cavalry meets a civilian-type Piper J-3-65 liaison aircraft, marked with the white cross of the exercises, pushed up to a gas pump at a roadside general store to refuel. The Piper has been hastily painted in olive drab – its civilian registration is still visible – and is marked with the 'grasshopper' insignia applied by Piper factory personnel who were supporting its use. Despite opposition by the Army Air Forces, army aviation played an important role in ground forces operations.

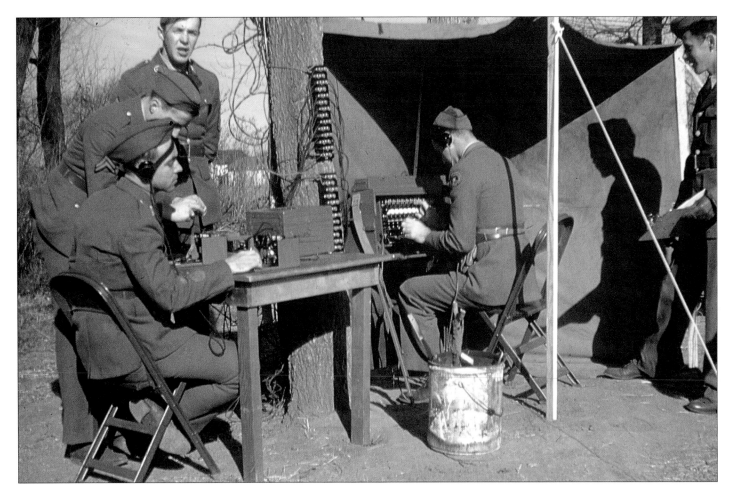

10. Although this photograph dates from 1942–43, all of the equipment and service uniforms, including the leather belts and brown shoes, were the same as pre-war. This was one of ROTC's attractions and, in the words of Paul Fussell; 'if you worked up to be a cadet officer, you got to wear a Sam Browne belt, from which depended a nifty saber'. Here, ROTC cadets at a college in the United States practise operating a field switchboard.

11. Prefabricated single-story tarpaper buildings of the 59th Fighter Squadron's operations area at Glenn L. Martin Airport, Maryland, along with a Chevrolet staff car, in August 1942. The transition from pre-war to wartime army was progressing as new posts were built and new units organized almost daily.

Learning
the New Warfare
Airborne, Armored, and Amphibious Operations

12. (previous page) The birth of the US Army Airborne forces. Paratroopers of the 502nd Parachute Battalion board a C-53 transport at Lawson Field, Fort Benning, Georgia, during the Carolina Maneuvers on 28 November 1941. The paratroopers wore two-piece prototype jump suits and did not carry their rifles when jumping (they were dropped in separate containers).

13. Other Services were also learning the new warfare. The 1st Marine Parachute Battalion learns parachute handling on the ground at Quantico, Virginia. The aircraft is a Navy Douglas R3D-2 transport, a military version of the unsuccessful DC-5 airliner, used for training in 1942. The Marine paratroopers never made a combat jump, but saw much heavy fighting – the 1st battalion was on Guadalcanal in 1942 – until they were disbanded for infantry replacements in 1944.

14. Trainee paratroops start to learn their trade on a jump tower at Fort Benning, 10 May 1943. The trainee is assuming the proper 'stand in the door' position, with his hands on the outside so that he can be easily shoved out if he should freeze. To the right of the trainee are static lines of previous jumpers. Attached to the aircraft and to the jumper's parachute, these used his weight to open the parachute automatically when he was a safe distance from the aircraft.

15. Paratroops at Fort Benning in May 1943 train on a mock-up C-47 fuselage (the broom propped against the 'fuselage' was not part of operational equipment). These paratroopers do not carry their weapons but are fully rigged for jumping, showing how close they would stay on leaving the aircraft, to try and avoid spreading the 'stick' of paratroops throughout the drop zone. The reserve chest parachute worn by each man is today universal, but the US Army was the first to introduce it during the Second World War. British paratroopers normally would not use a reserve parachute during operational jumps.

16. Marine paratroopers learn how to handle an opened parachute on the ground at Quantico, Virginia. The US Army organized five airborne divisions in the Second World War, the 82nd, 101st, 11th, 17th and 13th, as well as a number of non-divisional units. The Marines formed five battalions of paratroopers.

17. A paratrooper poses for the camera in front of a C-47 with his SCR-536 'handie-talkie' radio in 1943. Although this lightweight portable FM tactical radio often suffered from limited range and poor reliability ('optimistic in conception, quite hopeless in practice' was one former infantry officer's description), it was still a great advance over the portable radios used by allies and adversaries alike. Invented in the United States pre-war, the FM tactical radio made many of the new tactics possible.

18. A jeep of the 320th Field Artillery Battalion (Glider), 82nd Airborne Division, is unloaded from *The Mountaineer*, a Waco CG-4A transport glider, during train-ing in the United States. Because of the limitations of air-dropping – the doors of C-47 transport aircraft would barely accommodate bulky cargo such as a jeep – the US Army put great emphasis on the use of gliders to bring in the heavy equipment for airborne forces. The CG-4A had a wooden structure and was mass-produced largely by furniture manufacturers. It was often considered disposable once it had delivered its cargo. While the US Army used the larger, heavier British Airspeed Horsa glider to lift airborne division artillery in Europe, the CG-4A remained the work-horse throughout Europe and in the China-Burma-India (CBI) Theater.

19. The M4A4 Sherman tanks of the 40th Tank Battalion, of the 7th Armored Division, which was later to gain fame defending St. Vith in the Battle of the Bulge, maneuver in the California-Arizona exercise area on 5 October 1942. The pennants on radio antennas and the use of massed tank naval-style formations without the integration of armored infantry were changed after the defeats of US tank forces at the Kasserine Pass, Tunisia in 1943. The US Army only used the M4A4 for training, chiefly at the desert training Center, Indio, California.

20. *Doolittle,* an M4A4 on the same October 1942 maneuvers, requires help from an M3 half-track equipped with a generator; a jump start may be required. Each tank company's maintenance section had one such half-track.

21. M4A1 of D Company, 11th Tank Battalion, 10th Armored Division.

22. An M4 Sherman tank of the 10th Tank Battalion, 5th Armored Division, on exercises amidst spectacular foliage in 1943. The Sherman was the US Army's standard medium tank of the Second World War. Produced in large numbers and mechanically reliable, it was nevertheless deficient in armor, firepower and survivability when compared with many of its German opponents.

23. The crew of *Cowboy*, belonging to C Company, 11th Tank Battalion, 5th Armored Division, loads 75mm M48 high-explosive shells into their M4 Sherman during training in 1943. The word 'super' on the rounds they are handling indicates a propellant supercharge. The black-tipped rounds waiting to be loaded are M61 armor-piercing (AP) for use against armor and fortifications.

24. The US Army realized that armored warfare was not just about tanks, but required combined arms forces, including self-propelled (SP) artillery. US armored divisions each had three artillery battalions, each with 18 of these M7 105mm SP howitzers. The M7 also equipped non-divisional artillery battalions.

25. *Finalist*, an early production M7 105mm SP howitzer of the Armored School Demonstration Regiment training at Fort Knox, Kentucky, in 1943.

26. Another view of *Finalist*. The M7 was a stopgap design which used the chassis of the earlier M3 Grant medium tank and lacked overhead cover for its crew. Even the US Army, with its technically sophisticated fire-control systems and tactical communications, had problems in coordinating indirect howitzer fire with rapidly maneuvering armored forces.

27 (below). On exercise in California in 1943, this mobile combination laundry, shower and delousing station, constructed on a modified standard ten-ton box trailer towed by a five-ton truck, is an example of the specialized equipment evolved by the US Army. Equipment such as this underlines the US Army's emphasis on its logistic support 'tail', which, at the expense of requiring the allocation of considerable manpower and equipment away from the combat divisions, allowed them to be projected world-wide and sustained in combat. The drawback was that such equipment frequently did not reach the front-line troops. The 3rd Infantry Division was never provided with any bathing facilities at all during its first year in action. Bill Mauldin wrote; 'The infantryman bathes whenever he has the opportunity, which is about twice in summer and not quite as often in winter'.

28 (left). The July 1941 California maneuvers saw the army's early attempts to develop an amphibious capability. The 1st Infantry Division had initiated amphibious training off Puerto Rico earlier that year, making the first two of its many invasions. Within a few months after this exercise, the 3rd Infantry Division started amphibious training in Puget Sound and the mouth of the Columbia River. The techniques used in 1941 would appear primitive compared with those used in action. Here, a 37mm M3A1 anti-tank gun is lowered over the side of a pier into a waiting lighter, while its crew, with old-style M1917 helmets but new M1 Garand rifles, climb down a cargo net alongside. A fishing boat in the background underscores the fact that it is still peacetime.

29 (above). Infantrymen of the 53rd Infantry Regiment, 7th Infantry Division, training at Fort Ord, California, in March 1941 on an obstacle course that also helps teach how to climb down a cargo net from the deck of a transport into a landing craft. The diversity of uniforms suggests how difficult it was for the rapidly expanding army to clothe its soldiers. Most wear the M1938 model of the denim fatigue suits the army had used since the turn of the century with overseas caps, while others wear the pre-war campaign hat. Some wear the pre-war hot-weather two-piece light khaki chino service uniform, which proved unsuitable for combat conditions when worn by troops defending the Philippines in 1941–42. The 53rd Infantry was pulled out of the 7th Infantry Division before Pearl Harbor.

30. When training for amphibious operations, troops had to climb over the side of attack transports, using either specially constructed flexible ladders as shown here or simply cargo nets, into landing craft waiting alongside to take them to the beach. In actuality, with both vessels pitching and rolling, the troops heavily laden, everything wet with spray and almost everyone seasick, a mis-step often proved fatal. Extensive amphibious training helped the US Army develop formidable operational capability in an aspect on which, before the war, it had placed little emphasis.

The War Stateside

31 (previous page). A G.I. uses his government-issue mess kit and M1941 single-burner gasoline stove to prepare a meal (corned beef hash) during training. More compact M1942 'mountain stoves' and Primus stoves (purchased by the G.I.s themselves) were lighter. The United States Army of the Second World War certainly ate more, if not better, than both its allies and adversaries.

32. Maintenance in the field for a standard US Army Harley-Davidson WLA motorcycle in 1942. More than 60,000 WLA models were produced during the war. The widespread production of the jeep allowed it to take over many of the overseas roles originally intended for motorcycles.

33. Inflating the tires from a jeep and a trailer in front of a Diamond T 6x6 4-ton truck, using a portable compressor, 1942. The soldier in the foreground wears the old blue denim fatigue uniform under his green fatigue suit jacket. His tool roll, with each tool suitably labeled, is displayed nearby.

34. G.I.s wearing M1941 field jackets welding at a field maintenance shop, repairing a wheel, 1942. They have not yet been issued with M1 Garands; the rifles piled in the foreground are bolt-action M1917 Enfields.

35. Fort Benning, May 1945. An infantryman wearing the late pattern HBT (herringbone twill) fatigues poses for the camera, showing how it should be done, even with helmet strap fastened (rarely done in combat). The US Army's combat uniforms were diverse but frequently inadequate, especially in conditions of cold, wet, or heat. Similarly inadequate was the stateside training, often months behind lessons learned in combat.

36. The 58th Fighter Group ground echelon chow line on a wooded slope, on exercise in Rhode Island.

37. A pup tent bivouac during an exercise in Rhode Island. The G.I.s are wearing the M1942 one-piece herringbone twill fatigue overall and the pre-war M1940-pattern blue denim fatigues. Overseas, however, there were few pup tents in the front lines.

38. Soldiers of the US Army's Chemical Corps fill 100lb aircraft bombs with liquid chemical agent at Edgewood Arsenal, Maryland. The protective suit is the heavyweight version used only by personnel working with noxious chemicals, and was highly fatiguing to wear in hot weather. They carry the older-model triangular gas mask container under their arms and wear M3 gas masks. Chemical weapons were often stored in bulk, in containers such as the large drum from which the bombs are being filled. Large quantities of non-lethal chemical weapons ('tear gas') were used during training in the United States to teach defensive chemical warfare, vital if more lethal chemicals had been used in action.

39. An M2 flamethrower is demonstrated at the Edgewood Arsenal, Maryland, on 23 September 1944. The infantrymen are demonstrating the proper positioning for covering flamethrowers.

40. An M4 flamethrower tank with a bow-mounted M3-4-3 flamethrower demonstrates its firepower at Fort Benning in May 1945. It used unthickened fuel, leading to the large flame and short range apparent in the photograph. Flamethrower tanks were particularly invaluable in clearing out Japanese cave and bunker positions in the Pacific, and were an integral part of the 'corkscrew and blowtorch' tactics.

41. Colored smoke, here demonstrated by an M4A1 Sherman at the Edgewood Arsenal in 1943, was an invaluable wartime innovation, allowing troops to mark their position for supporting aircraft or other troops, thereby avoiding fratricide.

42. An M1 90mm anti-aircraft gun posing for the camera fires with the aid of a searchlight during training in the United States in 1944. By this period of the war, however, night-time firing was primarily done with radar. In any event, the searchlight would never have been so closely co-located with the guns, blinding the crews. A technically excellent design, the M1 was used as a field gun on several occasions in Europe.

43. It was widely known that there was nothing more dangerous than a second lieutenant with a map. Lieutenant Dennis Glen Cooper, wearing the 'pinks and greens', the green shirt and the 'pink' khaki trousers that were the officer's service dress in the Second World War, has his tie tucked into his officer's shirt (distinguished from that worn by enlisted men by its epaulettes), as required by regulations when the tie was worn without a jacket.

44. Mild mock humiliation of field-grade officers for the benefit of the camera at Ontario Army Air Field, California. That G.I.s tended to consider the manual peeling of potatoes an irksome task was a source of wonder to allies and enemies, who were less well fed and cherished any duty that brought them into contact with food. Later in the war, mechanical potato peelers and prisoners of war often performed this task.

The
Mediterranean Theater
North Africa, Sicily, and Italy

45. (previous page) Lieutenant General George S. Patton took over command of II Corps after its initial defeat at the Kasserine Pass in 1943. Patton had helped establish the US Army's armored forces in the WWI, leading them into battle in 1918. Before going overseas in the Second World War, he had helped mold the successful tactics that mechanized forces would employ throughout the war. After North Africa, a mixture of battlefield success, dynamic leadership and a flair for publicity and showmanship kept him in the public eye.

46. The Sicily campaign. Paratroopers of the 82nd Airborne Division gather up their parachutes and equipment. Despite the Allies' overwhelming numerical superiority –

more troops were involved in the initial invasion than would take part in the D-Day landings in 1944 – the Germans fought a skilful delaying action. The 82nd proved itself to be one of the best Allied infantry units in the fighting, despite suffering heavy losses to Allied naval anti-aircraft fire on the first day of the invasion as its incoming C-47s overflew the invasion fleet.

47. A Polish 40mm Bofors anti-aircraft gun uses the basement of a destroyed house as a gun pit near Monte Cassino in 1943. G.I.s arriving from the United States were soon aware that this was a coalition war effort. Only in the last 11 months of the war in Europe were there more US than British Commonwealth divisions in action.

48. In Italy, the US Army found itself fighting alongside a wide range of allies. The Polish 3rd Carpathian Rifle Division, part of the II (Polish) Corps at Monte Cassino, was equipped entirely by the British, including this 3in mortar and the crews' sheepskin vests. II (Polish) Corps was to fight alongside US troops to the end of the Italian campaign.

49. US Army anti-aircraft gunners in Italy load an M1 40mm Bofors gun. They were a vital defense in German air attacks, especially against the Anzio beachhead. When the German air threat finally faded out, these troops were quickly retrained as infantry and put into the front line, formed into a regiment-sized task force.

50. A US Army convoy crosses the 210ft engineer bridge erected over the River Serchio, north-west of Pisa, built during the advance towards the Gothic Line in September 1944. The Serchio valley was later the scene of the last major German counterattack in Italy, on 26 December 1944. It made some initial progress, but was finally repulsed.

51. Infantry waves at the camera on the outskirts of Rome in June 1944. They are walking in single file at the side of the road to leave the roadway free for vehicles. The men wear the olive drab woolen uniform and plain helmets associated with US infantry in the Italian theater, and are armed with M1 rifles, described by Patton as 'the finest battle implement ever devised'.

52. The 210ft engineer bridge over the River Serchio in Italy used H-20 box girder components. Heavier bridges used British-style Bailey Bridge components. The extensive German demolitions, the limited infrastructure, and the difficult terrain made the US Fifth Army in Italy heavily dependent on the capabilities of its engineers.

53. A dead German soldier, killed when the US 85th and 91st Infantry Divisions broke through the Gothic Line at Giogia in September 1944. Paul Fussell, the literary critic and former infantry officer, described dead German infantry 'with open eyes and greenish-white faces like marble, still clutching their rifles and machine-pistols in their seventeen-year-old hands, fixed where they had fallen'.

54. The 1st Armored Division, 'Old Ironsides', fought its way through Italy. This Sherman at Lucca, Italy, on 10 March 1945 has the crew's rations and extra equipment stored externally on the front of the tank. Many Shermans, throughout the war, were uparmored with sandbags, armor, or simply equipment stored in this way, evidence that their crews often considered them too lightly armored. By 1944 many of the 1st Armored's Shermans carried appliqué armor on their hulls and turrets.

55. The infantry complained that all the best hotels in Rome were immediately commandeered for headquarters personnel or the Army Air Force. The former Mussolini Youth Center in Rome was put to better use as an American Red Cross canteen soon after its liberation in June 1944. The Combat Infantryman Badges and the red bull insignia of the 34th Infantry Division identify the G.I.s as veterans of some of the Italian campaign's most intense fighting, including Monte Cassino. The CIB was – and remains, with the Purple Heart – a distinction invariably regarded with respect by even the most cynical soldier.

56. G.I.s of the 36th Infantry Division board an LST for amphibious training in Italy, May 1944. Originally a Texas National Guard formation, the 36th suffered heavy losses in the crossing of the Rapido river. Built up with replacements, it took part in the invasion of southern France and advanced into Germany as part of the Seventh Army.

57. Engineers of the 317th Engineer Battalion, 92nd Infantry Division, clearing mines at Viareggio, Italy, on 3 March 1945. Left to Right: T/5 Melvin Browder, PFC Lorenzo Cashe, PFC Parrish C. Wade, Private Amish Fleming. African-American-manned non-divisional engineer battalions were also used in many theaters, including the construction of the Alaska highway in 1942.

58. The SCR-625 mine detector being used by these engineers of the 317th Engineer Battalion, 92nd Infantry Division, to clear mines on the beach at Viareggio, Italy, on 3 March 1945 is an example of technology developed by Polish military engineers in 1942, which formed the basis for almost all subsequent mine-detector technology development. It could find any buried metal to a depth of about a foot.

59. These engineers of the 317th Engineer Battalion, 92nd Infantry Division, seen clearing mines at Viareggio, Italy, on 3 March 1945, were members of one the US Army's two predominantly African-American infantry divisions. The other was the 93rd, which served in the Pacific. A third African-American division, the 2nd Cavalry, also went overseas but was disbanded before seeing action. In the Second World War the army found that the policies of racial segregation it had applied since the Civil War were not only politically costly, but an appallingly inefficient use of human resources.

60. A German mine detonated by engineers of the 317th Engineer Battalion, 92nd Infantry Division, at Viareggio, Italy, on 3 March 1945, emphasizes the extensive use of mine warfare by the Germans as an economy-of-force measure, especially in Italy, where the fighting was frequently static with limited axes of advance. One track was found to have mines every eight paces for three miles.

61. An M4A1 Sherman tank of the 1st Armored Division near Pisa in January 1945. Improvised storage includes a large basket on the front fender, and foliage provides camouflage. In the words of the 1st's commander, Major General Ernest Harmon; 'The Sherman lacked the gun power of the German Tigers and Panthers, although I think it was mechanically superior. In the long run the measure tipped in our favor because our supply of tanks so far outran that available to the Germans.'

63. Air evacuation to Naples, 1944. A wounded G.I. is unloaded from a C-47 for travel by jeep to a nearby Army hospital. Watching the unloading, their work in the evacuation chain for the moment complete, are a flight nurse (in a blue flight suit) in the door of the C-47 and the aircraft's pilot (with the sunglasses and '50-mission crush' hat affected by many aircrew).

62. An M24 light tank of the 81st Reconnaissance Squadron, 1st Armored Division, moves through Vergato on 15 April 1945, on the way to liberate Bologna. The M24 was the ultimate wartime US light tank. Fast (35mph) and well-armed, with a lightweight 75mm M6 cannon, it saw extensive service in late 1944 and 1945. Dangling from the turret is a crewman's personal weapon, a .45 Thompson submachine-gun made more suitable for tank use by removing the stock, shortening the barrel and taping two magazines together.

64. Flight nurse Lieutenant Frances Sale checks on a casualty, PFC Raymond Lobell, wounded in the left shoulder, before he is loaded for the evacuation flight south to Naples in 1944. The US made extensive use of air evacuation of casualties. In Italy, C-47s would often fly into forward airstrips to evacuate casualties to hospitals at Naples or Foggia. Because of the damaged and traffic-clogged state of Italy's rail and road net, this obviously saved much time.

65. Victory in Italy. The city gates of Verona are still intact, and the city behind them shows little damage. A US Army Dodge ½ ton Command Car and a standard Dodge 4x4 ½-ton ambulance are in front of the gates.

66. Much of Italy was not as fortunate as Verona. Bill Mauldin commented; 'If there isn't much of a town left at all, then planes have been around'. Here a British military policeman, Lance Corporal J. C. Wood, allows a party of Italians carrying flour sacks to pass after the area has been checked for unexploded ordnance and mines.

67. A 'Whizz-Bang' crew of the 752nd Tank Battalion reads mail. The Rocket Launcher T40 (M17) held twenty 7.2in rockets in a metal box frame. They were electrically fired, singly or in salvoes, and the launcher was elevated hydraulically using the Sherman's 75mm-gun controls. The whole assembly could be jettisoned if required. Mounted on standard Sherman tanks, the Whizz-Bang saw limited combat use in 1944–45. The 752nd Tank Battalion was a non-divisional tank battalion that fought the length of Italy, supporting different infantry divisions.

68. April 1945; German vehicles and artillery pieces – including an 88mm anti-aircraft gun – and a freight train that obviously did not make the retreat northwards from the last Allied offensive in Italy. Both tactical airpower and Italian partisans inflicted heavy losses on the retreating Germans and their Italian allies (with whom the partisans often had scores to settle that transcended the immediate tactical situation).

69. Germans and Italians of Mussolini's puppet regime are held in a IV Corps PoW cage in April 1945 as the final Allied offensive causes the collapse of the opponents who had fought so tenaciously and skilfully up the 'boot' of Italy. Germans generally preferred to surrender to Americans, especially infantry, rather than to other Allies, and especially in preference to partisans.

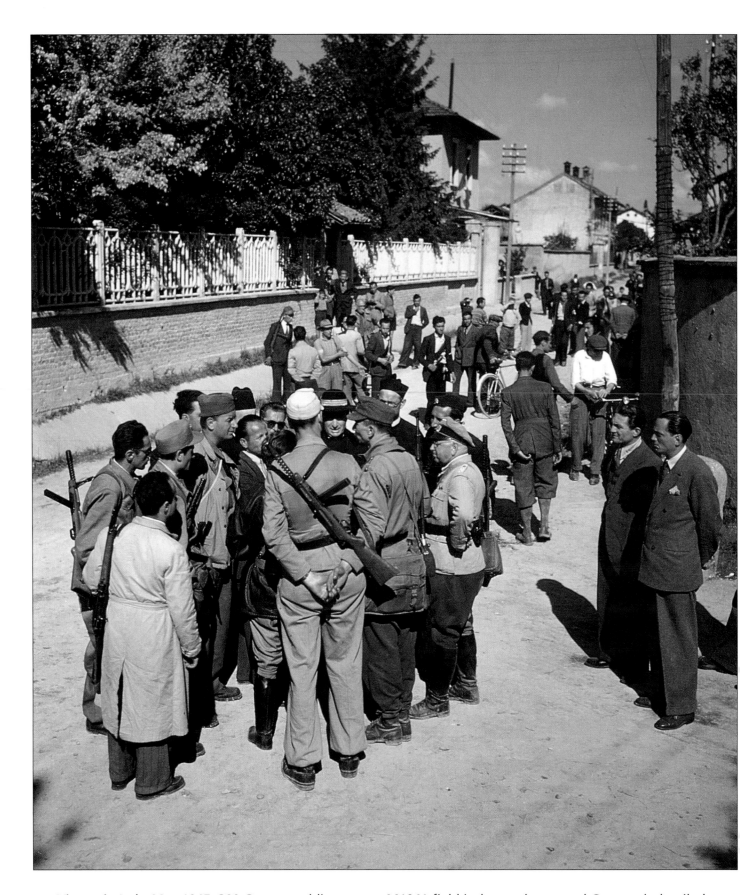

70. Victory in Italy, May 1945. 300 German soldiers are about to turn themselves over to the 1st Armored Division without firing a shot. The three still-armed German officers are negotiating their exit to a PoW cage with a US officer (wearing a light olive drab M1941 field jacket and captured German hobnailed mountain boots), the partisan leadership (on the left of the group) and the local religious leadership (the traditional biretta) accompanied by an Italian military chief chaplain (wearing the broad-brimmed hat).

The European Theater
Preparing for Battle

71 (previous page). Upon arriving in the European theater, many G.I.s found that their stateside training had not prepared them for the realities of modern warfare. There was much to learn from the British in the operational use of radar. This is a British 90cm searchlight mounted with a Searchlight Control (SLC) AA No.2 Mk 7 radar with Identification Friend or Foe (IFF) Mk 3 aerials. The radars would allow the searchlight to be aimed at enemy aircraft for visually directed anti-aircraft fire.

72. G.I.s soon found themselves all over England, often inserted into the life of the countryside and its people. Here, two G.I.s in service dress walk down the high street of Eye, in Suffolk, which has been dressed in flags, either to celebrate a victory or for a village fete.

73. Many G.I.s, such as the two reclining on the grass in the center, also in service dress, found wartime London a great if crowded place to work or visit, despite shortages and hardships.

75. An M7 105mm SP howitzer fires during training. There was less opportunity for live fire training in England compared with the United States, one reason why many US divisions were held in the States and brought over after D-Day. The muzzle blast and smoke of the M7's short howitzer were considerable.

76. Amphibious training, seen here on 29 December 1943, was carried on both in Europe and along the coast of the United States. An M4A1 Sherman comes ashore from the USS *LST* (Landing Ship Tank) *262*, itself in a two-toned camouflage scheme. Amphibious training itself could be dangerous. On the night of 27-28 April 1944, three LSTs were torpedoed by German motor torpedo boats off Slapton Sands in Lyme Bay, with the loss of 197 sailors and 441 soldiers.

74. (above) An M1 flamethrower being demonstrated in training in the ETO. The paratrooper wears an experimental M1942 jump suit that was a forerunner of the herringbone twill suit introduced in Normandy – including to the 30th Infantry Division and the 17th Engineer Battalion of the 2nd Armored Division – in 1944, and soon withdrawn after soldiers wearing them were misidentified as Waffen SS. The M1 was heavy (about 70lb) but produced up to 10 sec of flame at up to 30 yards range. It was extensively used by combat engineers against enemy fortified positions.

77. Waiting for the invasion in England in 1944, US armored infantrymen Corporal John Hartlage, Corporal Edward Smith and Private George Roberts pose for the camera with their M3A1 halftrack. One is perusing the Army's 'teach yourself French' paperback. The M3 half-track, armed with an M2 .50-caliber machine-gun, was mechanically reliable but thinly armored – infantrymen called them 'Purple Heart boxes' – and too slow over rough ground to keep up with M4 tanks. The tube on the vehicle's right running to the engine is to prevent it from being drowned while coming ashore.

78. The USS *LST 262* lands another M4A1 Sherman, this one apparently with a joint-service crew. On D-Day the Shermans were unable to land directly on the beach from LSTs. Instead, amphibious 'Duplex Drive' Shermans were launched from LSTs to swim ashore. In the rough seas, most sank on their way to the beach.

79. The crew of USS *LST 49* watches a 57mm anti-tank gun with its WC-62 (with winch) Dodge 6x6 1½-ton truck and crew load aboard
The officer in the foreground is obviously a natty dresser, with his trousers, boots and polished helmet setting him apart from the G.I.s. Such distinctions were against the provisions of the army dress regulations (AR 600-35), and they were not maintained in action for obvious reasons.

80. The 1st Infantry Division training for D-Day, Weymouth, 1 May 1944. The British LCAs (Landing Craft Assault) in the foreground – the smallest type of Royal Navy landing craft – carried the initial assault waves. In the background are the larger US LCIs (Landing Craft Infantry) that carried the later waves.

81. G.I.s of the 1st Infantry Division board US Navy LCVPs (Landing Craft Vehicles and Personnel) for amphibious training, Weymouth, 1 May 1944. The LCVPs were used in the same way as the British LCAs, but were more seaworthy. While the LCIs would sail under their own power to Normandy, the LCAs and LCVPs were hoisted on to the davits of assault transports.

82. The *Big Red One* loading while training in preparation for D-Day, Weymouth, 1 May 1944. Sailors watch as troops of the 1st Infantry Division back a GMC 2½-ton truck on to an LST down a ramp specifically built for loading troops.

The 1st Infantry Division was involved in many of the European theater's invasions: North Africa, Sicily, Salerno, and finally D-Day.

85. A WAC (Women's Army Corps) crane operator (wearing their wartime 'Hobby hat' headgear) lifts a spare vehicle tread into a waiting truck at an ordnance installation. Piles of vehicle tracks lie on both sides of the crane, named *Dinosaur*, one of several types used for a variety of ordnance tasks, including lifting bombs. A total of 140,000 women served in the army during the Second World War, 17,000 of them overseas.

83 (far left). US-manned LCVPs with G.I.s of the 1st Infantry Division alongside the Esplanade at Weymouth, in training for D-Day, 1 May 1944. They are literally waiting 'for the balloon to go up', as three inflated barrage balloons are on the ground in front of the ornate facade of the Weymouth Pavilion (burned down in 1954). The balloons would be attached to landing craft for low-level air defense, although they were sometimes jettisoned on D-Day because they tended to draw fire.

84. The balloon goes up. Many of the Allied landing craft in the D-Day invasion had barrage balloons flying above them with steel cables to deter attacks by low-flying enemy aircraft. US Army barrage balloon units were ashore in Normandy by the close of D-Day, and were used as part of the anti-aircraft defenses in Europe throughout the rest of the war. Barrage balloons proved effective against V1 flying bomb attacks.

86. A Dodge WC 52 ¾-ton 4x4 weapons carrier and a DUKW 2½-ton amphibious truck wait to load aboard the USS *LST 357*. Over 1,000 LSTs were eventually built in the United States, one of the great triumphs of industrial mobilization.

The European Theater
D-Day and the Liberation of France

87. (previous page) G.I.s pose on the beachhead for the camera with mail from home; the T-5 on the right wears the shoulder patch of Army engineer amphibian units.

89. A jeep is loaded into a C-47 transport of the Ninth Air Force at an airfield in England after D-Day. Although its antenna has been removed for loading, this jeep is fitted with VHF radio equipment for air-ground communication. Such VHF-equipped jeeps made improved air-ground cooperation with the Ninth Air Force's fighter groups possible throughout the 1944–45 campaigns.

88. A German PoW cage on the beaches at Normandy. The prisoners are waiting to be loaded aboard the LSTs unloading vehicles and supplies over the beach, for the trip back to a permanent camp in Britain or the United States.

90. The liberation of Dinard, in Brittany, August 1944. PFC Walter T. Stankowski of the 121st Infantry Regiment, 8th Infantry Division, checks out a local inhabitant who turned out to be friendly and had refused evacuation. Stankowski is armed with a standard M1 Garand rifle.

91. A mortar squad of the 83rd Infantry Division poses for the camera during the fighting at St. Malo in Brittany, August 1944. These 'plumbers' are bringing up a 60mm M2 mortar, the infantry's standard company-level support weapon, which fired mainly high-explosive and illumination rounds. They were the company commander's 'vest pocket artillery'.

93. The invasion of southern France, 18 August 1944. DUKW amphibious truck *Beaufighter* of Company B, the 52nd Quartermaster Battalion, ferries supplies ashore. It is armed with a .50-caliber machine-gun on a ring mount, originally fitted to only a quarter of all DUKWs. Free French troops have already hoisted their flag as the French First Army comes ashore to join in the liberation.

92. A US M1 40mm anti-aircraft gun positioned to overlook St. Malo, France. The absence of cables running to the mount show that the gun is relying on local control and has not yet been hooked into its battery fire control director, the normal mode of operation. However, one of the crew has found time to do the laundry. The M1 was the US-produced version of the basic Swedish-designed Bofors gun, replacing the US-designed 37mm M1A2. US Army anti-aircraft batteries defended targets such as Antwerp, Liege and Remagen bridge against aircraft and V1 flying bombs in 1944–45, while many of these units' personnel were retrained as infantry replacements.

94. The devastation of war was seen everywhere by G.I.s in France, but was seldom more spectacular than at Toulon, where the remains of the French fleet lays scuttled to avoid capture in 1942. The gutted remains of the battleship *Strasbourg*, against Jetty 6 of the Quai Milhaud, has been partly scrapped by the Germans.

95. Despite being harassed by Allied airpower and French resistance fighters, much of the German Nineteenth Army defending southern France still managed to escape encirclement at Montelimar. However, 57,000 prisoners were taken. A 105mm FH 18/40 light howitzer, recognizable by its light spoked wheels, is among the debris.

96. The remains of a German horse-drawn 105mm howitzer battery lies pushed off to the side of the road at Montelimar on 28 August 1944. Meanwhile, troops of the US Seventh Army move past in pursuit of the escaping remnants of the Nineteenth Army, heading towards the Rhine.

97. Wounded G.I.s were not only airlifted to medical care more often than their allied or enemy counterparts, but medical support could be airlifted to them in-theater. After D-Day, Noorduyn UC-64 Norseman transports, often used for high-priority intra-theater transport missions (one disappeared carrying bandleader Glenn Miller on his way to a concert in Paris on 16 December 1944), were also used to fly fresh blood where needed in an unprecedented example of medical organization. In this picture, probably posed for an in-theater blood drive, whole blood is being loaded aboard a waiting Dodge ambulance.

98. On 25 August 1944 came the long-awaited liberation of Paris. The liberators were the French 2nd Armored Division under General Jacques Le Clerc. These US-built M3 half-tracks are from that division, its well-known insignia, an outline of an undivided France (Hitler having re-annexed Alsace and Lorraine) with the cross of Lorraine superimposed, being visible on the fenders. The rebuilt Free French Army was equipped primarily with US weapons. This photograph was taken the following day, 26 August, as General De Gaulle returned to Paris.

99. The US Army learned from the British about specialized armored vehicles such as this modified 'Aunt Jemima' M4 Sherman of the 25th Armored Engineer Battalion, crossing the River Moselle north-west of Nancy. Its T1E3 (M1) mine exploder was intended to detonate anti-tank mines, and the heavy rollers were designed to survive multiple mine detonations. Because of its weight, it sometimes needed two M4s pushing in tandem.

100. The specialized 'Aunt Jemima' equipment developed in 1943 replaced an earlier mine exploder designated 'The Pancake'. Each of its two roller units comprised five 10ft-diameter steel disks driven from the M4's front sprockets. One example of the US Army's engineering equipment was the 254-ton steel pontoon treadway bridge it is on.

101. Three Ninth Air Force junior NCOs in liberated Paris share beers at the Café George V with a T/5 who is armed with a .45-caliber pistol.
The AAF personnel wear helmets and are armed with the more practical M1 carbine. This establishment had obviously managed to preserve its Allied flags in hiding throughout the German occupation.

102. Other G.I.s in Paris include, far right, a T/5 artilleryman from the 36th Infantry Division. This photograph was obviously taken after the preceding one, as no one is carrying weapons or wearing a helmet. Even during the heavy fighting of 1944–45, much of the US infantry found itself constantly in the line and away from Paris or any rest at all. An average of one man per infantry company received a pass every month.

The European Theater
The Battle of the Bulge and the Defeat of Germany

103 (previous page) The distinctive ivory-handled revolvers worn at the hip and the USAAF flying jacket identify this figure – even from behind – as LTG George S. Patton. Patton's Third Army was able to respond quickly to the German offensive in the Ardennes and his counterattack against the southern flank of the "Bulge" to relieve the besieged defenders of Bastogne was one of the campaign's most successful actions.

104. A dismounted patrol from Company C, 48th Armored Infantry Battalion, 7th Armored Division in St. Vith, Belgium, during the later stages of the Battle of the Bulge, January 1945. The white camouflage overalls were in short supply and were frequently improvised locally, often from mattress covers. The US Army, for all its logistical capability, often failed miserably in delivering suitable winter clothing to front-line troops in the winter of 1944–45.

105. 60mm mortarmen of Company C, 23rd Armored Infantry Battalion, moving dismounted outside St. Vith during the Battle of the Bulge. The 7th Armored, reinforced by infantry units and individual G.I.s falling back from the flanks, succeeded in blocking the advance of much of Sixth Panzer Army in December 1944. In January 1945 it participated in the counterattack that recaptured St. Vith, when this photograph was taken.

107. While the Battle of the Bulge was being fought to the north, there was also heavy fighting further to the south (shown by the height of the mountains in the background) in France. Lieutenant Fred Merritt of the 645th Tank Destroyer Battalion prepares to open fire with his M36 tank destroyer against German positions on the Seventh Army front on 20 December 1944.

106. M4 Shermans of the 40th Tank Battalion, 7th Armored Division, during the Battle of the Bulge. The 7th Armored finally withdrew from St. Vith on 23 December to avoid encirclement and shorten Allied lines. By that time, however, the weather had started to clear and, to the south, the relief of Bastogne had started. The 7th Armored remained in the Ardennes until after St. Vith was recaptured in January 1945. This photograph was taken on 24 January 1945.

108. One of the best-known incidents of the Battle of the Bulge was the near-hysteria caused by the discovery of German infiltrators dressed in US Army uniforms. Sergeant A. Para checks the identification of a Belgian farmer in the town of Namur at the north-western edge of the Ardennes. In the background is Hitler's objective in the Bulge; the Meuse River.

109. The bolt-action M1903 'Springfield' rifle, shown here with a telescopic sight and front sights removed, was the standard US Army sniper rifle throughout the war. Sergeant Douglas Dillard, a paratrooper of the 551th Parachute Infantry, was photographed on the Seventh Army front on 20 December 1944. The battalion, which had airdropped as part of the invasion of southern France, later suffered the heaviest casualties of any airborne battalion in the Battle of the Bulge. Attached to the 82nd Airborne Division in December and January, the 551st was disbanded in February 1945. Sergeant Dillard survived to attend the 50th anniversary celebrations of his airdrop into France.

110. The results of victory. A German Panzer V Panther medium tank, knocked out and abandoned at the side of the road, shows the marks of a violent fire and explosion. While the Panther was individually superior to the US Army's M4 Sherman, it lacked their numbers or mechanical reliability. In the last months of the war, German tanks were frequently found abandoned owing to fuel shortages. CPT Edward Bautz, who served in the 4th Armored Division, recalled, 'We were outgunned by the German Mark V. The Mark IVs, we could handle in pretty good shape. The Mark Vs had a high velocity 75. We had a little edge on them in maneuverability, but they had more armor protection.'

III. Troops of the 3rd Battalion, 194th Infantry (Glider), 17th Airborne Division securing the rail line north of Wesel during Operation Varsity on 25 March 1945, the day after the Allied airborne crossing of the Rhine. Parachutes from the resupply airdrop are still hanging in trees. The glider pilot from the 98th Squadron, 440th Troop Carrier Group, smoking a cigarette in the foreground (with a first aid package attached to his helmet netting) is armed with an M1928A1 .45 Thompson submachine-gun. Other glider pilots and troopers have British-pattern airborne folding bicycles for local mobility. In the middle background another is using a supply canister as a backrest.

112. In the evening of 24 March the first resupply DUKWs which had swum across the Rhine behind the assault troops linked up with the 3rd Battalion, 194th Infantry (Glider) and 98th Squadron glider pilots. More DUKWs followed on the morning of the 25th, as shown here. The 25th saw more hard fighting as they linked up with the rest of the 17th Airborne, and after that they advanced to the east, capturing Münster. The two days which opened the fighting of Operation Varsity cost the 17th Airborne 393 dead, 834 wounded and 80 missing, many of the casualties resulting from crashed gliders.

113. Over the Rhine to victory. Troops of the US Seventh Army roll over the Alexander Patch Bridge, named for their commanding general, on 28 March 1945. This heavy pontoon bridge was built by the 85th Construction Engineer Battalion. The Seventh Army was the last of the US armies to cross the Rhine.

114. Company F, 2nd Battalion, 325th Infantry (Glider), 82nd Airborne Division, demonstrates urban combat in Germany. The exploding white phosphorus grenade appears genuine, but the discarded portrait of Hitler in the foreground and the fact that the veteran paratroopers are kneeling in the middle of the street rather than hugging cover shows that this is a posed photograph. The airborne divisions were frequently kept in action longer than they should have been because they represented some of the best US Army infantry in the ETO.

The Pacific and China-Burma-India Theaters

The War Against Japan

115 (previous page). Fighting on Bougainville, 1943. By this time the army was starting to learn the 'corkscrew and blowtorch' tactics against Japanese defenders in caves or bunkers, using flamethrowers or demolition charges to knock them out while covered by as much firepower as possible, and, when terrain permitted, close support by tanks.

117. Unloading supplies on the island of Amchitka in the Aleutians, 23 July 1942. Massive barges full of supplies were tugged up from the continental United States. Here they are being offloaded over the beaches by a mixed force of soldiers and sailors, assisted by civilian-model logging tractors and a mobile crane.

116. After the Japanese invaded Attu and Kiska in June 1942, the Provisional Tank Company, Fort Glen, Unimak, Alaska, at the base of the Aleutian chain, was equipped with Marmon-Herrington T16 light tanks (originally built for Netherlands East Indies), armed with three .30-caliber machine-guns. Fortunately, these tanks were not put into action before they were relegated to training.

118. Troopers of the 1st Cavalry Division pose on an M5A1 (with later hull and rounded flat-top turret without bustle) light tank. The US Army was aware of the importance of close infantry/tank cooperation throughout the Pacific fighting. The 1st Cavalry saw heavy fighting in the Admiralty Islands (where army and Australian M3s and M5s provided much of their armor support in the difficult terrain), and in the liberation of the Philippines.

119 (top right) LVT-2 amphibious tractors used for training, Guadalcanal, 1944. Following the lead of the Marine Corps, the US Army formed numerous battalions of amphibious tractors for Pacific operations. These included armored versions, the armament including 75mm howitzers and flamethrowers.

120. Watching artillery fire hitting Japanese positions on Saipan, 8 July 1944. Saipan was the largest and most decisive ground combat of the Marianas campaign, giving the US forces airbases within striking range of Japan.

121. Marines, armed with M1 carbines, on Saipan on 8 July 1944, with M4 Shermans in the background. The camouflaged helmet cover was a common Marine Corps item. The Sherman proved important throughout the Pacific fighting, Lieutenant General Mitsuru Ushijima writing; 'The enemy's battle power lies in his tanks. It has become obvious that our general battle against American forces is a battle against their M4 tanks.'

122. Saipan, 7 July 1944. A Marine on the crest of the hill looks at artillery fire impacting on the last Japanese line of resistance in the rugged north of the island. Resistance ended, after desperate counterattacks followed by mass suicides, on 9 July 1944. The command relationships on Saipan were marred by recriminations between army and marine generals.

123. At sea aboard an LSD (Landing Ship Dock) of the invasion force the day before the invasion of Morotai, 14 September 1944. Action is not anticipated, as the LSD's anti-aircraft guns are covered up. The LSD will flood its center well and launch the LCVPs carrying troops of the 31st and 32nd Infantry Divisions. Airbase construction provided the capability to strike north to the southern Philippines or west to the Netherlands East Indies.

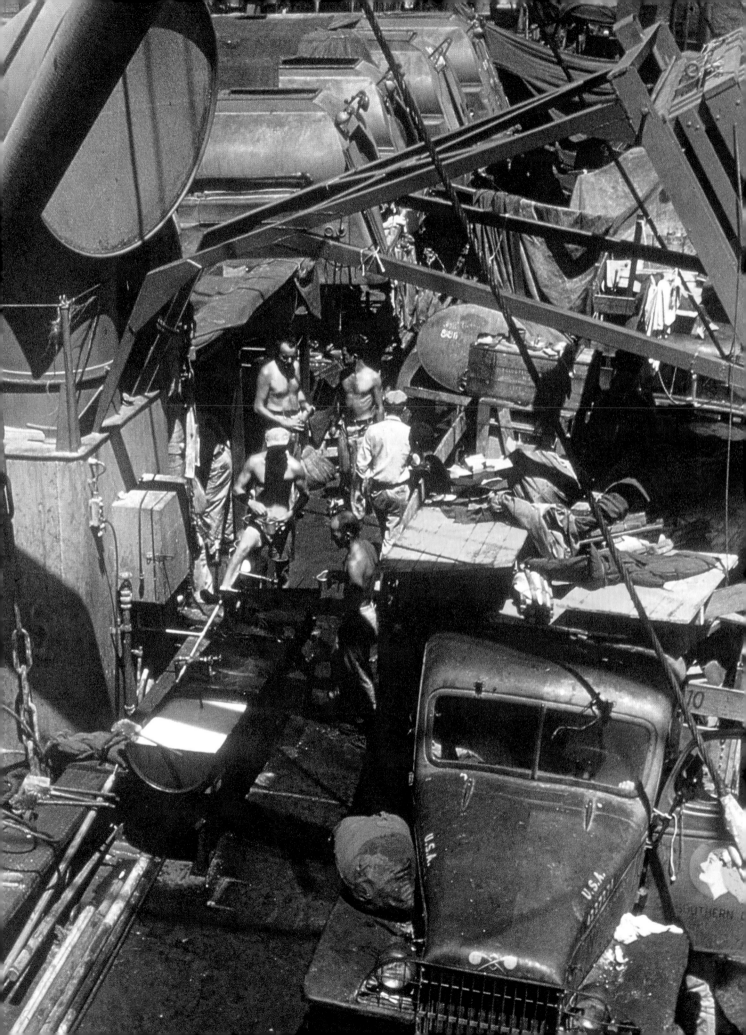

124. Aboard the *Morrsion R.*, a transport bringing Army troops from New Guinea to the Philippines. The early-model 2½-ton truck (most had been withdrawn from front-line units by the time this photograph was taken in 1944) in the foreground has the twin-retorts insignia of the Chemical Corps on its hood and a personal insignia on an open door. The Army Air Force's ability to paint elaborate names and personal insignias on its airplanes was seldom able to be imitated by the ground forces.

125. A dinner of corned beef hash, mixed vegetables and tinned peaches is enjoyed from a G.I. messkit on board the Liberty ship *Russell Sage* sailing between New Guinea and the Philippines. The messkits came either with a two-compartment lid, as shown here, or with a single compartment. The diner wears a faded olive drab M1941 short-visored HBT cap, often condemned as unsoldierly in appearance stateside, but practical in tropical conditions.

126. An M3A1 37mm anti-tank gun of the 129th Infantry Regiment, 37th Division, opens fire on Japanese positions west of the Intramuros district in Manila. While it proved too light to be effective in its intended role as an anti-tank gun in Europe, the 37mm was used in the Pacific throughout the war, not only against the lighter Japanese tanks, but also as an effective infantry support weapon, often using high-explosive or canister rounds.

127. Shaving by feel, without the G.I.-issue steel shaving mirror, on board the Liberty ship *Russell Sage* sailing between New Guinea and the Philippines.

129. A fire-blackened cinema after the liberation of Manila shows evidence of the intensity of the fighting. Sergeant H. N. Oliphant witnessed it; 'Manila was burning. The whole downtown section was smothered in roaring black billows of smoke. The Jap shells were coming in.'

128. Devastation after house-to-house fighting in Manila. The 37th Infantry Division carried out some of the most sustained urban combat of the war in downtown Manila during February-March 1945.

130. Outdoor dining area, Lingayen, the Philippines. Such facilities were a rarity for combat troops, although support and Army Air Force units had more opportunity to set them up. On the whole, G.I.s in the Pacific Theater of Operations ate much less well than those in Europe, in terms of both quantity and quality of food.

131 (top right). Baseball became the American national sport in wartime – the Civil War – and every Pacific island out of the line of fire soon sprouted multiple baseball diamonds like this one on Saipan in 1945. Japanese stragglers, in the hills, would also watch the games.

132. Sunset at Tacloban, on Leyte in the Philippines. Wartime experience brought Americans face to face with sights and peoples that appeared strange to citizens of a country which was much more insular fifty years ago than it is today.

133. A GMC 2½-ton truck with an American flag flying from its fender encounters a muddy road near Dulag on Leyte in the Philippines. The rain in the Philippines fell in sheets, while that on Okinawa was a cold, incessant drizzle.

134. While no US Army combat divisions were committed to the China-Burma-India (CBI) theater against Japan, there were many other army combat and support units, as well as the Army Air Force, in the theater. These Chinese Army troops, about to board a C-47 for the trip back over 'the Hump' to China, had been flown out of China to north-east India, where they had been equipped and trained by the US Army.

135. In addition to the C-47s – here, one belonging to the USAAF and one to the Chinese Air Force – there were units of every branch of the US Army in the CBI Theater. General Stilwell, the senior army ground soldier in the theater, was relieved in 1944 following tension between the Chinese government and Army Air Forces leaders who would, in retrospect, validate 'Vinegar Joe's' view.

136. Rainy season in the 17th Reconnaissance (Bomb) Squadron enlisted men's area at Finschafen, New Guinea. Throughout the Pacific theater, the US Army found itself fighting weather conditions as much as the enemy.

137. A column of M4A3 Shermans from the 6th Marine Division move up a dirt road on Okinawa, 6 May 1945. Both Army and Marine Corps M4s were vital in the slow, bloody infantry attacks that marked much of the fighting on Okinawa. The tank battalions suffered heavy losses to mines, anti-tank guns and suicide squads using hand-carried demolition charges. Fortunately, tank-infantry cooperation had evolved to a high degree by this stage of the war. Many tank crews had several M4s shot out from under them on Okinawa without suffering any personnel casualties.

138. The fighting on Okinawa, as on Guadalcanal, Saipan, and in many of the other key battles of the Pacific War, brought G.I.s into action alongside Marines. While there was some tension at the command level, there was a highly evolved system of cooperation among the fighting men. Here, Marines of the 6th Marine Division are moving up on 6 May 1945 in a convoy that includes both Army and Marine Corps trucks.

139. August 1945, the island of Ie Shima, off Okinawa. By this time Ie Shima was a large US airbase. The ships off-shore were bringing in supplies for the build-up preceding Operation Olympic, the planned invasion of Japan.

140 (top right). A tented camp on Ie Shima in the summer of 1945. A generator for the 17th Reconnaissance (Bomb) Squadron photographic laboratory is being unpacked from shipping crates in the foreground.

141. 29 July 1945: a forklift loads equipment from a standard GMC 2½-ton truck on to a C-46 transport for a flight to Ie Shima. The C-46 provided valuable logistic support, but it was distrusted by paratroops because of its tendency to burn if hit by ground fire.

142. How many G.I.s went home from the Pacific war by being delivered to C-54 transports like these on Guam by 4 x 4 Dodge WC 54 ¾-ton ambulances such as this one?

143. Significant numbers of civilians were victims of the fighting on Okinawa. The massive US use of firepower and the Japanese disregard for their safety led to high civilian casualties which are still remembered on Okinawa to this day. Here, the official US Army photographer records three soldiers conducting an old woman to the rear.

Victory and Homecoming

144 (previous page). The US 69th Infantry Division had the first meeting with the Red Army at Torgau on 25 April 1945. Private Billy Zeep, PFC Orrie Diker, PFC Marion Wampler and PFC Paul A. Alenburg pose with a Soviet soldier. Female soldiers in combat units were a novelty to the Americans. To the Soviets, the American's equipment was a wonder, though they found the M1 rifle too heavy for their liking.

145. First Lieutenant Dwight Brooks, commanding some of the first troops to meet the Soviets, with his Red Army counterparts. Even in the first days of the inspirational meeting it was apparent to the G.I.s that the seeds of the Cold War were being planted. Sergeant Allan Ecker wrote; 'It doesn't take a second look to know the Russians are planning to stick around for a while in Germany. In our area, American flags are few and far between, mostly on military-government offices, but over on the Russian side almost every window of the occupied town buildings flies a red flag...'

146. Major General Emil E. Reinhardt of Decatur, Georgia, commanding the 69th Infantry Division, meets his Soviet counterpart, Major General V. V. Rusakov, commanding the 58th Guards Rifle Division, Fifth Guards Army, First Ukrainian Front, 26 miles north-east of Torgau on 26 April 1945.

147. US national mythology insists on victory and requires that it be symbolized with massive parades at the end of a war. Here, General Mark Clark takes the salute at a massive Allied review at the Monza auto track in Italy to mark the victory in May 1945. The troops are the 1/11th Anti-Tank Regiment, 6th South African Armored Division, but their equipment is the US-produced M10 tank destroyer armed with a 3-inch gun, known as the Wolverine in British Commonwealth service.

148. An infantryman of the 10th (Mountain) Infantry Division prepares to leave Italy after the war. The 10th was the only specialist mountain division to be formed and go overseas in the Second World War. Its personnel included some of the United States' foremost skiers and mountaineers. After extensive training stateside, it was finally committed to combat in Italy, and spearheaded much of the US Fifth Army's final advance in 1945.

149. 'I hereby declare these proceedings closed' were the words with which General of the Army Douglas MacArthur ended the surrender ceremony on the deck of the battle-ship USS *Missouri* in Tokyo Bay on 1 September 1945. A Navy band struck up 'California, Here I Come'. Standing by are the Allied signatories to the documents of surrender: Admiral Sir Bruce Fraser, representing Great Britain; General Kuzma Derevyanko, representing the Soviet Union; General Sir Thomas Blamey, representing Australia; Colonel Lawrence Moore-Cosgrave, representing Canada; General Jacques Le Clerc, representing France; Admiral Conrad Hel-ferrich, representing the Netherlands; and Air Vice Marshal L. M. Isitt, representing New Zealand.

150. Still functioning after the victory were the US Army's stateside hospitals. This is a well-lit Nissen hut ward of the 65th General Hospital. With demobilization, the US Veteran's Administration hospital took over the massive task of treating and rehabilitating injured and sick military personnel.

151. The end of the journey for many who served in the European Theater of Operations; the three-funneled RMS *Queen Mary* in the Hudson River (opposite the Lincoln Tunnel ventilation towers at 38th Street in Manhattan) is about to be tugged alongside the pier. *Queen Mary*, along with the other great Cunard liner of the era, RMS *Queen Elizabeth*, played a vital role in moving the US Army overseas to England. Up to 16,000 soldiers were packed aboard the big troopships, which traveled without escort in mid-ocean. The loss by fire of the comparable French liner *Normandie* in the Hudson while being converted to a troopship in 1942 delayed the build-up of US forces in England. Despite the cramped accommodation, those who traveled home on the big liners thought themselves luckier than those who had to go by six-knot Liberty ships.

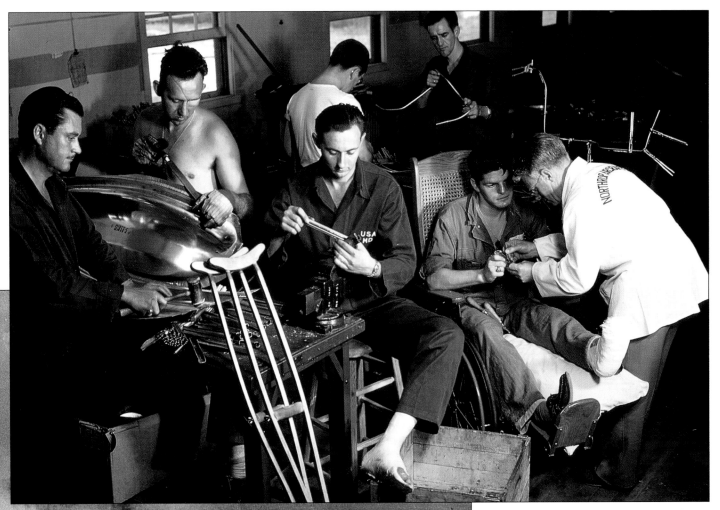

152. During the war, patients at an Army hospital combine vocational rehabilitation for a post-service career with making a contribution to the war effort. An instructor from Northrop Aircraft teaches metalworking.

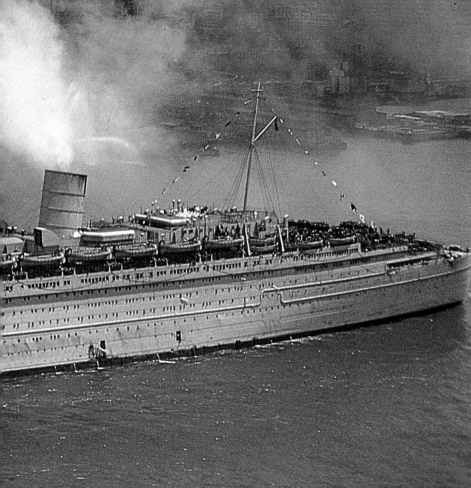

153. For those waiting for the ship home (or waiting to go to the Pacific Theater for the invasion of Japan) there were tours and entertainment. With a flak tower and a gutted hangar for a backdrop at Nordholz, a former German air-base near Bremen, comedian Bob Hope and his troupe are on stage. Hope's mixture of comedians, showgirls and musicians remained constant throughout the Second World War, Korea, Vietnam and the Cold War, being altered only for the Gulf War in deference to Saudi sensibilities.

154. The victorious G.I.s soon became the first post-war American tourists in Europe, either unofficially as duty permitted or through officially organized groups. Here, a group of the 4th Armored Division, 'Patton's Best', passes through a piece of countryside untouched by war.

155. At the end of the Gulf War in 1991, one G.I., sorting out a crowd of Iraqi prisoners, turned to a buddy and reminded him; 'You know, of course, this means that in 50 years we'll all be driving Iraqi-made automobiles'. A traditional Japanese ox-cart, its driver's baseball-style fatigue cap being one of the few usable inheritances from the Imperial Japanese Army, was frequently encountered on the roads by the first occupation troops.